MONSTER MADNESS

# THE STORY OF MEDUSA

ANNA COLLINS

Enslow PUBLISHING

**Please visit our website, www.enslow.com. For a free color catalog of all our high-quality books, call toll free 1-800-398-2504 or fax 1-877-980-4454.**

**Cataloging-in-Publication Data**
Names: Collins, Anna.
Title: The story of Medusa / Anna Collins.
Description: New York : Enslow Publishing, 2023. | Series: Monster madness | Includes glossary and index.
Identifiers: ISBN 9781978531727 (pbk.) | ISBN 9781978531741 (library bound) | ISBN 9781978531734 (6pack) | ISBN 9781978531758 (ebook)
Subjects: LCSH: Medusa (Gorgon)–Juvenile literature.
Classification: LCC BL820.M38 C65 2023 | DDC 398.20938'01–dc23

Published in 2023 by
**Enslow Publishing**
29 E. 21st Street
New York, NY 10010



Designer: Tanya Dellaccio
Editor: Jennifer Lombardo

Photo credits: Cover Alexander_P/Shutterstock.com; p. 5 (statue) Volodja1984/Shutterstock.com; p. 5 (Athena) Prachaya Roekdeethaweesab/Shutterstock.com; p. 7 (gold statue) 80's Child/Shutterstock.com; p. 7 (carving) Marco.Warm/Shutterstock.com; p. 9 (Medusa) Tame69/Shutterstock.com; p. 9 (jellyfish) Arzu Kerimli/Shutterstock.com; p. 11 (all) Masterlevsha/Shutterstock.com; p. 13 (statue) pandapaw/Shutterstock.com; pp. 13, 17 (illustrations) delcarmat/Shutterstock.com; p. 15 (Pegasus) Warpaint/Shutterstock.com; p. 15 (statue) Luc Emergo/Shutterstock.com; p. 17 (statue) Ullrich Gnoth/Alamy Images; p. 19 (roof tile) Artokoloro/Alamy Images; p. 19 (evil eye) Marish/Shutterstock.com; p. 19 (limestone carving) Dima Moroz/Shutterstock.com; p. 21 (illustration) Natalia Tan/Shutterstock.com; p. 21 (statue) Beatrice Sirinuntananon/Shutterstock.com.



Printed in the United States of America

# CONTENTS



**Boldface** words appear in the glossary.

# WHO IS MEDUSA?

The ancient Greeks told a story of three **mythical** sisters called Gorgons. Their names were Euryale, Stheno, and Medusa. When they were born, Euryale and Stheno looked like monsters, but Medusa looked like a beautiful human woman. The first two were also **immortal**, but Medusa wasn't.

The story goes that the sea god Poseidon saw how beautiful Medusa was. He wanted to kiss her so badly that he did it without asking her in the goddess Athena's temple. Athena saw this and got angry that her temple wasn't being respected.

THE GODDESS ATHENA **CURSED** MEDUSA.

## BELIEVE IT OR NOT!

ATHENA WAS THE ANCIENT GREEK GODDESS OF WISDOM AND WAR. HER TEMPLE WAS SUPPOSED TO BE A PLACE FOR PEOPLE TO HONOR HER. WHEN POSEIDON HURT MEDUSA, IT DIDN'T HAVE ANYTHING TO DO WITH HONORING ATHENA.

# MADE INTO A MONSTER

Even though Medusa didn't want to kiss Poseidon, she was the one Athena **punished**. Athena did this by turning Medusa into a monster like the other Gorgons. Different stories have different **descriptions** of Medusa. Some say she had wings and scales. Others say she had a beard and sharp teeth. A few say she also had a giant boar's tooth sticking out of her mouth.

There are two things all the descriptions share: Her hair turned into snakes, and she gained the power to turn people to stone by looking at them.

THIS LIKENESS OF MEDUSA IS IN SAXONY, GERMANY.

**BELIEVE IT OR NOT!**

MEDUSA'S POWER IS CALLED PETRIFICATION. SOMETHING THAT'S BEEN PETRIFIED HAS BEEN TURNED TO STONE. PETRIFIED CAN ALSO MEAN VERY SCARED—SO SCARED THAT YOU FEEL LIKE YOU CAN'T MOVE, AS IF YOU'VE BEEN TURNED TO STONE!

# WHO IS PERSEUS?

Perseus was another mythical figure. He was the son of the god Zeus and a mortal woman named Danaë. When Perseus was a baby, Danaë's father sent the two of them away because an **oracle** had told him he would one day be killed by his grandson.

Danaë and Perseus ended up on the island of Seriphus, which was ruled by King Polydectes. King Polydectes wanted to marry Danaë, but she didn't want to marry him. Perseus kept Polydectes away to **protect** his mother. Polydectes decided he had to get rid of Perseus.

THE SCIENTIFIC NAME FOR AN ADULT JELLYFISH IS A MEDUSA BECAUSE THE TENTACLES REMIND PEOPLE OF SNAKES.

# PERSEUS ON THE HUNT

Polydectes pretended to be marrying someone else and held a great feast. Everyone who was invited had to bring a gift. Perseus was too poor to give anything. Polydectes told Perseus he had to make things right by bringing him Medusa's head. He was sure Perseus would die trying.

Athena and another god named Hermes gave Perseus some magic things that would make it easier for him to kill Medusa. One of these was a cap that belonged to the god Hades. It made anyone who wore it **invisible**.

# GREEK AND ROMAN MYTHOLOGICAL FIGURES

THE ROMANS HAD MANY OF THE SAME GODS AND MYTHS AS THE GREEKS, BUT THE NAMES WERE OFTEN DIFFERENT IN LATIN.

MEDOUSA/MEDUSA

HADES/PLUTO

ZEUS/JUPITER

ATHENA/MINERVA

HERMES/MERCURY

POSEIDON/NEPTUNE

## BELIEVE IT OR NOT!

PERSEUS WAS ALSO GIVEN HERMES'S WINGED SANDALS AS WELL AS SOME HELPFUL THINGS THAT WEREN'T MAGICAL. THESE WERE A SICKLE, OR CURVED SWORD, TO CUT OFF MEDUSA'S HEAD; A BAG TO PUT THE HEAD IN; AND A SHINY METAL **SHIELD**.

# KILLING MEDUSA

Perseus went to the island where the Gorgons lived. The shield Athena had given him was so shiny that he could use it as a mirror. This kept him from looking directly at Medusa and being petrified. He cut her head off while she slept and put it in the bag so he wouldn't accidentally see it on the way home.

When the other Gorgons found out Medusa was dead, they tried to chase after Perseus. However, he was wearing Hades's cap of invisibility, so they couldn't find him.

## BELIEVE IT OR NOT!

AN ANCIENT GREEK POET NAMED PINDAR WROTE THAT THE GORGONS WENT BACK TO THEIR CAVE AND CRIED FOR MEDUSA. ATHENA HEARD THEIR CRIES AND MADE A MUSICAL INSTRUMENT CALLED THE AULOS THAT SOUNDED JUST LIKE THEM.

PERSEUS IS SHOWN HERE HOLDING UP MEDUSA'S HEAD.

# STILL POWERFUL

Medusa's body was still powerful after she was killed. When Perseus cut her head off, her two sons were born from her neck. Their names were Chrysaor and Pegasus. Pegasus was an immortal winged horse. He is much better known today than Chrysaor is.

Perseus flew home using his winged sandals. On the way, he found a princess named Andromeda. Her parents had chained her to a rock to be eaten by a sea monster as a **sacrifice** to Poseidon. Perseus used Medusa's head to petrify the monster. He saved Andromeda and married her.

PEGASUS WAS ONE OF MEDUSA'S CHILDREN.

ASCLEPIUS

## BELIEVE IT OR NOT!

GREEK POETS WROTE THAT MEDUSA'S BLOOD HAD POWERS, TOO. THE BLOOD FROM HER LEFT SIDE COULD KILL PEOPLE, AND THE BLOOD FROM HER RIGHT SIDE COULD BRING THEM BACK TO LIFE. IT WAS USED BY ASCLEPIUS, THE GREEK GOD OF MEDICINE.

# WHAT HAPPENED TO THE HEAD?

When he finally got home, Perseus petrified Polydectes with Medusa's head to save his mother from marrying him. Most stories say he later gave the head to Athena. She put it on Zeus's **aegis**. Stories said Medusa's head would roar when Athena went into battle.

Some writers say that Perseus didn't give Athena the head. Instead, he went back to his birthplace of Argos with Danaë and Andromeda. These stories say he buried the head in the marketplace.

SHOWN HERE IS ATHENA WITH THE AEGIS.

**BELIEVE IT OR NOT!**

THE ANCIENT GREEKS SAW PICTURES IN THE STARS THAT THEY CALLED CONSTELLATIONS. THEY BELIEVED THE GODS PUT THEM THERE TO TEACH PEOPLE LESSONS. THERE ARE CONSTELLATIONS NAMED AFTER PERSEUS, ANDROMEDA, PEGASUS, AND MANY MORE GREEK MYTHS.

# A SIGN OF PROTECTION

Because Medusa is so often shown as just a head, the head has its own name. It's called the gorgoneion. Over time, the gorgoneion became a **symbol** of protection to the ancient Greeks. It has been found on ancient buildings, vases, shields, special necklaces called amulets, and many other things.

The idea was that this scary and powerful monster would scare away evil. This would protect whoever owned the thing that had her face on it. In fact, the name Medusa comes from the ancient Greek word for guardian.

THIS IS A GORGONEION ON AN ANCIENT ROOF TILE.

THIS GORGONEION IS **CARVED** IN LIMESTONE.

## BELIEVE IT OR NOT!

GREEKS HAVE USED ANOTHER PROTECTION SYMBOL FOR MANY YEARS. IT'S CALLED AN EVIL EYE AMULET, AND IT LOOKS A LITTLE LIKE A BLUE EYE. PEOPLE BELIEVE IT STOPS OTHER PEOPLE FROM CURSING THEM WITH A MEAN LOOK.

# MEDUSA TODAY

People have started to question Medusa's myth. They want to know why Athena punished Medusa instead of Poseidon. They don't think it's fair to say Medusa was a monster when she didn't really do anything wrong.

Some people are imagining the story differently. When this happens with an old myth or fairy tale, it's called a retelling. Modern retellings of Medusa's story often spend more time on her than on Perseus. They also talk about how Athena's decision was unfair.

MODERN PICTURES OF MEDUSA OFTEN SHOW HER WITH A BEAUTIFUL FACE.

## BELIEVE IT OR NOT!

IN 2019, A GROUP OF PEOPLE PUT ON A PLAY ABOUT A RETELLING OF THE MEDUSA MYTH. IN THIS PLAY, ATHENA ISN'T PUNISHING MEDUSA. INSTEAD, SHE'S GIVING HER THE POWER TO STOP PEOPLE FROM HURTING HER AGAIN BY PETRIFYING THEM.

# GLOSSARY

**aegis:** A shield that was associated with Zeus and Athena.

**carve:** To make or get by cutting.

**cursed:** Magical words that are said to cause trouble or bad luck for someone.

**description:** A written or spoken statement about something that helps a person picture it.

**immortal:** Never dying.

**invisible:** Unable to be seen.

**mythical:** Like a legend or story.

**oracle:** An ancient Greek priestess who told the future.

**protect:** To keep safe.

**punish:** To make suffer because of a wrongdoing.

**sacrifice:** The act of killing as an offering to please a god.

**shield:** A piece of metal or wood used to guard the body in battle.

**symbol:** A picture, shape, or object that stands for something else.

# FOR MORE INFORMATION

## BOOKS

Johnson, Hal, and Tim Sievert. *The Big Book of Monsters: The Creepiest Creatures from Classic Literature*. New York, NY: Workman Publishing, 2019.

Menzies, Jean, and Katie Ponder. *Greek Myths: Meet the Heroes and Heroines, Monsters and Gods of Ancient Greece*. New York, NY: DK Publishing, 2020.

Ward, Marchella, and Sander Berg. *A Journey Through Greek Myths*. London, UK: Flying Eye Books, 2020.

## WEBSITES

**Cleveland Art Museum**

*www.clevelandart.org/art/2021.3*

Take a look at this ancient gorgoneion roof tile that was found in southern Italy.

**Ducksters: Monsters and Creatures of Greek Mythology**

*ducksters.com/history/ancient_greece/monsters_and_creatures_of_greek_mythology.php*

Want more monstrous creatures? Check out this website!

# INDEX